Loyola University Chicago

Kathryn A. Young and Ashley Howdeshell

The Campus History Series

LOYOLA UNIVERSITY CHICAGO

KATHRYN A. YOUNG AND ASHLEY HOWDESHELL

ARCADIA
PUBLISHING

Published by Arcadia Publishing
Charleston, South Carolina

Library of Congress Control Number: 2020937885

For all general information, please contact Arcadia Publishing:
Telephone 843-853-2070
Fax 843-853-0044
E-mail sales@arcadiapublishing.com
For customer service and orders:
Toll-Free 1-888-313-2665

Visit us on the Internet at www.arcadiapublishing.com

This book is dedicated to the generations of students, staff, faculty, and alumni that have made Loyola University Chicago what it is today.

CONTENTS

Acknowledgments   6

Introduction   7

1.   Father Damen's Dream   9

2.   Home on the Lake   17

3.   Downtown College to Water Tower Campus   53

4.   Creating a Medical Campus   69

5.   A Campus in the Eternal City   97

6.   Loyola in the 21st Century   109

Bibliography   126

Index   127

ACKNOWLEDGMENTS

A university archives photograph collection could not be assembled without the talents of the photographers whose work ends up in the collection. The photograph collection at the Loyola University Chicago Archives & Special Collections is no different. The authors would like to thank the many photographers, most of whom are unidentified, who have worked for Loyola University Chicago over the last century and a half. Without them, it would not have been possible to create this book. We would especially like to acknowledge the late Thomas J. Dyba; Thomas J. Bryant, SJ; and Joe Smajo, whose photographs are extensively used in this book. Other known photographers in the collection include the St. Ignatius Camera Club, A.P. Risser, Morrison of Chicago, Grignon, Pontiac Photographers, James E. O'Brien, Mark Beane, Heather McNeill, Natalie Battaglia, Chris Strong, Katie Wall, Jim Young, Giulio Napolitano, and Lukas Keapproth.

The authors would like to thank James S. Prehn, SJ, EdD, vice president and special advisor to the president for mission and identity; Janet W. Sisler, vice president for mission integration; Jeremy Langford, vice president for marketing and communication; and the rest of Loyola's sesquicentennial committee for their support of this project. We would also like to thank Dr. Kyle Roberts and Dr. Justin Hastings for their willingness to read and comment on the manuscript.

Finally, we would like to thank our colleagues in the university libraries as well as our student workers for their patience, understanding, and support while we worked on this book.

Unless otherwise noted, all images appear courtesy of the Loyola University Chicago Archives & Special Collections.

INTRODUCTION

For 150 years, Loyola University of Chicago has grown with the city of Chicago, educating and serving its populace and assisting in times of disaster. Originally a one-building campus, the university now has three campuses in Chicago and one in Rome, Italy. Throughout the 19th and 20th centuries, the size and location of these campuses changed, reflecting the needs of a burgeoning city and university. Buildings have been constructed, demolished, and replaced as Loyola changed from a commuter school to a residential school and from a local college to an international university. All four campuses tell the story of Loyola University Chicago through their buildings and the students who have used them. The images in this volume help tell some of these stories.

When St. Ignatius College opened its doors on September 5, 1870, there were 37 students, the desks had just arrived, and the building was unfinished. Rev. Fr. Arnold J. Damen of the Society of Jesus (SJ) had decided to build his school on the western edge of Chicago, a growing area with an influx of immigrants. St. Ignatius College provided the children of these immigrants the opportunity of a high school and college education while also preparing them to be active citizens of the United States. Both high school and college classes were held in one building, a system that worked well until the end of the 19th century.

By 1900, enrollment in the high school division outpaced enrollment in the college division of St. Ignatius College. As the school grew, there was talk of establishing a division of the high school on the north side of Chicago, a growing area of the city and one to which many previous west-side residents were moving. It was during Rev. Fr. Henry J. Dumbach, SJ's, tenure as president (1900–1908) that the decision was made to pursue this course. In 1906, a total of 19.5 acres were purchased on the north edge of Chicago, and a north-side high school, Loyola Academy, was established. Recognizing the need for a larger college, Father Dumbach oversaw the separation of the college division from the high school division, resulting in the issuance of a new charter by the State of Illinois for Loyola University. The new university was soon established on the north side, sharing a campus with Loyola Academy. For the first decade and a half of its existence, the campus was designated the North Campus to distinguish it from the original campus on the west side. It was not until 1927 that a suggestion was made that the designation be changed to Lake Shore Campus, the name by which the main campus of Loyola University Chicago is known today. The next 114 years saw an expansion of the campus both in terms of buildings and land as well as an expansion of the Rogers Park neighborhood.

While the main campus of Loyola University Chicago was underway, other new campuses were beginning to emerge. The new charter allowed Loyola to establish professional schools, which it undertook to do. The first professional school was the School of Law, soon followed by the School of Medicine, the School of Sociology, and the Dental School. The addition of these schools, taught by professionals, required a campus in downtown Chicago. Located originally on what was known as the Ashland Block, the campus moved twice as additional professional schools were established, once to Franklin Street and then to its final home at what would become known as the Water Tower Campus due to its location next to Chicago's historic water tower. Over the next 74 years, the Water Tower Campus grew from one academic building to six, including a dormitory. Buildings that once existed, such as Siedenberg Hall and Marquette Center, were demolished and replaced, while other buildings were built on parking lots. Today, Water Tower Campus remains the home of Loyola's professional schools, but also serves as the home for several undergraduate programs. Due to this, Water Tower Campus has developed its own campus life separate from that of the Lake Shore Campus.

The Medical Campus has undergone many changes during the last 110 years. Originally consisting of only the medical and dental schools, this campus was first located in Chicago's medical district near Cook County Hospital. The School of Medicine was at 706 South Wolcott Avenue (then Lincoln Street), while the Dental School was on the corner of Harrison and Wood Streets. Both schools stayed at these locations until the Health Sciences Campus was established in Maywood, Illinois, on a site containing a former auto racetrack and the airplane runway used by Charles Lindbergh for delivering the mail. Loyola University Chicago purchased this 62-acre campus in 1961 from the Hines Veterans Administration Hospital; by 1969, the Stritch School of Medicine, School of Dentistry, and School of Nursing had relocated to the Health Sciences Campus in Maywood. The School of Dentistry closed in 1993, but the Health Sciences Campus continues to be the home of an expanded Stritch School of Medicine, Niehoff School of Nursing, Cardinal Bernardin Cancer Center, and the Center for Translational Research and Education.

The past half-century has seen Loyola University Chicago become not only a nationally recognized university, but an international one. During the tenure of Rev. Fr. James F. Maguire, SJ, from 1955 to 1970, Loyola established the first permanent American university campus in Rome—the Loyola University Chicago Rome Center for Liberal Arts. As with many of Loyola's other campuses, the Rome Center moved several times after its establishment. Former hospitals and convents hosted the Rome Center from 1966 to 1978, when it moved to its present campus. Rev. Fr. Michael J. Garanzini, SJ, president of Loyola from 2001 to 2015, ended the roaming of the Rome Center in 2009 when Loyola purchased the current campus on Monte Mario and renamed it the John Felice Rome Center. Now residing in a permanent home, the Rome Center is focused on providing one of the best international study programs in the world.

One

FATHER DAMEN'S DREAM

When St. Ignatius College opened its doors on September 5, 1870, it was the culmination of over a decade's worth of work in Chicago by Arnold J. Damen, SJ. In 1856, Chicago's Bishop Anthony O'Reagan invited the Missouri Province of the Society of Jesus to establish a Jesuit presence in the city after being impressed by Father Damen's missions. Father Damen was sent to Chicago and established Holy Family Church in 1857 on the west side, an area with an influx of Irish and German immigrants and near where Jacques Marquette, SJ, wintered in 1674–1675. He then worked on establishing primary schools for boys and girls, a precursor to a Jesuit higher education system in Chicago culminating in a college. A new school, St. Ignatius College, became the embodiment of that goal.

Father Damen purchased land next to Holy Family Church stretching west to Blue Island Avenue and north to Eleventh Street for the college campus. Through the efforts of alderman John Comiskey, father of Charles Comiskey of Chicago White Sox fame, a petition to close Aberdeen Street, which ran through the land purchased by Damen, was passed by the city council. This enabled Damen to begin building St. Ignatius College in 1869 with a unified parcel of land for the campus. Opening for classes on September 5, 1870, to male students only, St. Ignatius College became a place where students from many different backgrounds learned and interacted. Following the Great Chicago Fire of 1871, both the college and Holy Family Church became a refuge for people who were left homeless, including many members of religious orders.

On September 5, 1870, St. Ignatius College opened its doors to Chicago for the first time. According to the opening entry in the vice president's diary, the college building was still incomplete, although there were enough rooms finished to begin classes. Twenty-six students started the classical course, nine were in the commercial course, and two were in the preparatory course.

While conducting a series of missions in Chicago, Arnold Damen, SJ, so impressed the bishop of Chicago, the Right Rev. Anthony O'Reagan, that he requested Father Damen be assigned to the city to establish a Jesuit church and schools. This photograph shows Father Damen (seated second from left) along with several other Jesuits who traveled to Chicago with him to establish Holy Family Church and its related schools.

Founded in 1857 by Arnold Damen, SJ, Holy Family Church soon became the heart of a growing community. The first church was a wooden structure built for $1,600; however, construction of a stone Gothic cathedral featuring the work of German immigrant artisans was soon begun. Soon, several primary schools were established to serve the Holy Family community.

This picture, taken by the St. Ignatius College Camera Club, shows the interior of Holy Family Church in 1895. Although the Great Chicago Fire started only a few blocks away from Holy Family Church and St. Ignatius College, both were spared the flames and became a place of shelter for those who lost everything, including the archbishop of Chicago.

The first course catalog of St. Ignatius College was issued for the 1870–1871 school year and listed seven faculty members teaching two courses, the classical course and the commercial course of studies. Tuition for a school year, which ran from September to June, was $60, equivalent to $1,228 in 2020.

A scientific course was offered at St. Ignatius College beginning in the 1890s, following the long history of Jesuit education in the sciences. Students learned chemistry, physics, and the natural sciences and had access to a natural history museum and mineralogy collection. Some of the specimens from St. Ignatius College became part of the collections at the Field Museum of Natural History and Benedictine University.

Equipment for the science course was kept in cabinets in a room that was known as the "physical cabinet." This room was located next to the generator room and was used to run physics experiments. The students in this photograph are checking their equipment under the watchful eye of their Jesuit instructor.

The blackboard in this lecture room announces an upcoming lecture and demonstration on X-rays at St. Ignatius College on February 25, 1896. The Jesuit faculty of St. Ignatius kept track of current scientific theory and breakthroughs and often presented them in public lectures for the education of the community, in addition to classroom lectures.

St. Ignatius College was home to two libraries: the students' library and the main, or House, library. The students' library served the everyday needs of the students and included works such as grammar and literature. The House library was reserved for the Jesuit faculty and included numerous works on theology and philosophy in addition to the classics. Permission was sometimes given to exceptional students to use the House library. When Loyola University moved from the St. Ignatius College building to the north-side campus, many books from both libraries were relocated. Approximately 2,000 volumes remain in the Loyola University Libraries collection, some of which can be found in the rare book collection.

St. Ignatius College originally offered a six-year course with a focus on either the classics or commercial studies. In 1877, Fr. Rudolph J. Meyer, SJ, reorganized the structure and divided the course between grammar school, the equivalent to high school, and college. In addition, a scientific course was added to the classical and commercial courses. A further reorganization occurred at the end of the 19th century to meet national standards.

Traditional Jesuit education based on the *Ratio Studiorum* required that Jesuit schools provide a way for students to exercise and practice rhetorical self-expression. This was most often done through drama and debate, with several of each occurring throughout the scholastic year. During the 1904–1905 school year, the students of St. Ignatius College performed several plays, including *King Robert of Sicily*.

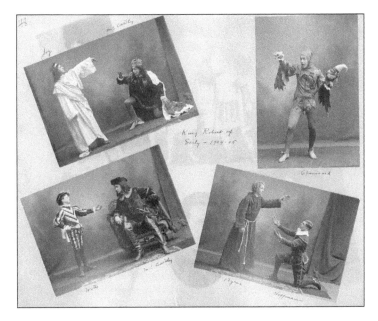

Physical education was recognized as an important part of education in the 19th century. The St. Ignatius College gymnasium included some of the latest gymnastic equipment, and exhibitions were a frequent occurrence. This tradition continued after the college department moved north to Rogers Park, when a gymnasium featuring the best swimming pool in Chicago during the 1920s was built.

Students at St. Ignatius College grew up with baseball. First abhorred by the Jesuit faculty for distracting students from their studies, it was eventually accepted and encouraged as an athletic activity. Baseball continued as a collegiate sport at Loyola University until it was discontinued in 1924. It is still played at Loyola as an intramural sport, however.

Two

HOME ON THE LAKE

One hundred and fourteen years will bring many changes to an institution and the place it calls home. After 36 years in the original St. Ignatius College building, Henry Dumbach, SJ, president of St Ignatius College from 1900–1908, decided that it was time to expand. In 1906, he purchased 19.5 acres of land for $161,000 in the neighborhood now known as Rogers Park, thus beginning Loyola University Chicago's Lake Shore Campus. While it was Father Dumbach who purchased the land for the new campus, it would be up to succeeding presidents to build it. The first buildings on campus were constructed during the tenure of Alexander J. Burrowes, SJ. Serving as president from 1908 to 1912, Burrowes oversaw the construction of Dumbach Hall and Cudahy Science Hall. Dumbach Hall was the home for the new north-side high school division, Loyola Academy, from 1908 until 1957, when it moved to Wilmette, Illinois. The second building, Cudahy Science Hall, was the first to host college classes. Alumni Gymnasium and the Administration Building arrived during the tenure of William H. Agnew, SJ, president from 1921 to 1927. Following the construction of these buildings, Loyola University was ready to move from the west-side campus at Eleventh Street and Roosevelt Road to the north-side campus.

Cudahy Library was built during the tenure of Robert M. Kelley, SJ, president from 1927 to 1933, and the Madonna della Strada Chapel was built while Samuel K. Wilson, SJ, was president, from 1933 to 1942. The presidencies of James F. Maguire, SJ, 1955–1970, and Raymond C. Baumhart, SJ, 1970–1993, saw expansions that included dormitories, classroom buildings, and a basketball arena. The most significant event during this time was the merger of Mundelein College with Loyola University, which expanded the main part of the campus to its current border of Devon Avenue on the south, Sheridan Road on the west, and Loyola Avenue on the north.

Seen here in his office at St. Ignatius College is Henry Dumbach, SJ, the 11th president of St. Ignatius College and first president of Loyola University. Father Dumbach purchased 19.5 acres in the Cape Hayes area on the north side of Chicago as the home of a north-side high school and college. He also oversaw the creation of the College of Arts and Sciences and the School of Law.

After months of negotiations with the Chicago, Milwaukee, and St. Paul Railway Company, Father Dumbach's offer for the north shore property was accepted and finalized in 1906. The railroad company retained the right of way for train tracks, thus creating the not-quite-uniform tract of land that became Loyola's main campus.

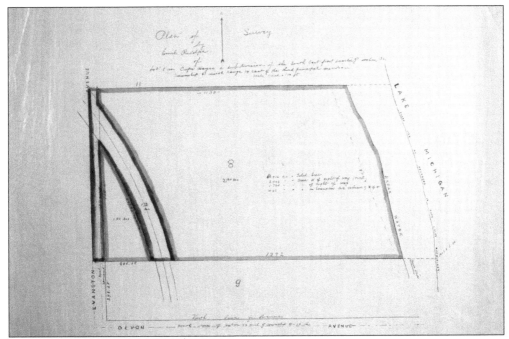

Several land surveys and plats were drawn up during the early part of the 20th century in order to establish the boundaries of Loyola University. This plat by Emil Rudolph was created in approximately 1920 and shows Loyola's campus in the subdivision known as Cape Hayes, later called Rogers Park. Shown on the plat are Devon Avenue and Evanston Avenue, which was later renamed Sheridan Road.

The 1908 course catalog contains one of the first sketches of the proposed north-side campus. The building that became Dumbach Hall, which was under construction when this sketch was done, is shown here with the original St. Ignatius Church in their correct locations on campus. The proposed future buildings all share a uniform Mission-style architecture.

One of the first structures built on the new north-side campus was the wooden-frame St. Ignatius Church, home of a new Jesuit parish. Built in 1907, this church was on Sheridan Road near Devon Avenue. It served the student population as well as a growing neighborhood until a new St. Ignatius Church opened its doors on Glenwood Avenue in 1917.

The interior of the first St. Ignatius Church was simple, with a main altar and side altars dedicated to the Virgin Mary and St. Joseph. Simple decorations were installed for celebrations such as Christmas and Easter. Fr. David M. Johnson, SJ, was the first pastor of the church.

This 1908 photograph shows the area in the Cape Hayes division that would become Loyola's Lake Shore Campus. Prior to the construction of Dumbach Hall, the area consisted of sand dunes, scrub, and beach. The beach was often covered by Lake Michigan's ebb and flow, which would bring in debris and litter.

At the same time that the land was purchased for Loyola's north campus, the Cape Hayes area became a desirable location for homes. Located near the growing town of Evanston, Illinois, but with easy access to downtown Chicago, Cape Hayes saw an influx of population. In order to create more lakeside land for homes, a seawall was built and filled with sand and dirt dredged from the bottom of the lake.

Building right next to a great lake can have consequences including flooding, such as seen in this photograph of the lawn in front of the Administration Building. A revetment project was begun in the 1950s and has been added to over the years to protect the shoreline from erosion and prevent floods.

Dumbach Hall, named for Henry J. Dumbach, SJ, first president of Loyola University, and the first academic building on the Lake Shore Campus, was built in 1908. This photograph shows an almost complete exterior of Dumbach along with the building that was known by students as "the boat house." At the front stands the foundation of Albert and Cassie Wheeler's house, known today as Piper Hall.

Designed by architect Paul V. Hyland in the Mission style, Dumbach Hall was constructed to be the new north-side high school, Loyola Academy. An all-boys school, Loyola Academy continued the St. Ignatius College tradition of educating the sons of Chicago regardless of their race, ethnicity, or religion. Loyola Academy remained at the Lake Shore Campus until 1957, when it moved to Wilmette.

The first Loyola Academy class of 1909–1910 established a long-running tradition of class photographs being taken on the steps of Dumbach Hall in front of the main door. Class photographs often included Jesuit faculty members in addition to the students. Loyola Academy athletic teams, including the baseball and football teams, as well as casts for the plays performed at the school, followed this tradition.

In 1921, Ferdinand Foch, supreme Allied commander during World War I, received an honorary degree from Loyola. He is seen here in front of Dumbach Hall, accompanied by William H. Agnew, SJ, Loyola president from 1921 to 1927. Behind Father Agnew is William T. Kane, SJ, who served as a chaplain for the 35th division of the US Army during the war and later as the librarian of Loyola University.

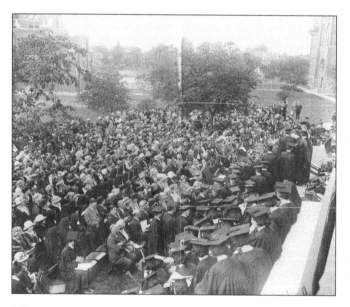

Commencement ceremonies were often held on the Lake Shore Campus in front of Dumbach Hall. This 1928 photograph shows students receiving their degrees with their families and friends watching. By this time, women were a fixture in the professional schools at Loyola and received their diplomas during the same commencement as male students. In the background, one can see houses where Mundelein College would eventually stand.

Built in 1912 and named for the co-founder of the Cudahy Meat Packing Company and Chicago philanthropist Micahel Cudahy, the Michael Cudahy Science Hall was the first building to host college courses on the Lake Shore Campus. Once completed, science courses moved to the north-side campus while the humanities remained at St. Ignatius College. Due to a lack of money, a telescope was never installed in the observatory dome.

Following the realization that the university would never be able to afford to install a telescope in the observatory of Cudahy Science Hall, a series of proposals was made on what to do with the dome. One of these proposals would have added decorations making the dome look more like a crown. Implementing this proposal was estimated at $3,000, the equivalent of $61,600 in 2020.

Kenmore Avenue once ran through Loyola's campus. Running north from Devon Avenue to Loyola Avenue, the road separated Cudahy Science Hall and Dumbach Hall from the athletic field and Alumni Gym. While this allowed for easier campus deliveries, it also provided neighborhood drivers with a frequently hazardous shortcut to Devon Avenue. This stretch of Kenmore Avenue was closed in the early 2000s in order to create the west quad.

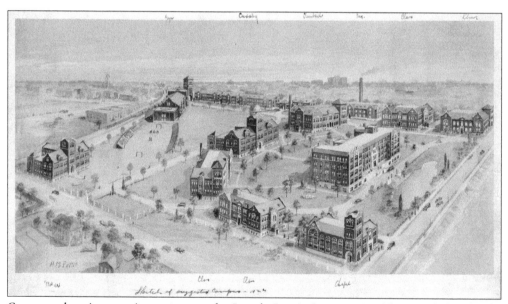

Campus planning was important to the Loyola Jesuit Community. This 1924 sketch of a proposed campus plan by H.M. Pettit shows campus buildings in the preferred Mission style. Four existing buildings—Dumbach Hall, Cudahy Science Hall, the Administration Building, and Alumni Gym—are on the sketch, which also shows the anticipated extension of Lake Shore Drive to Evanston.

The construction of the Administration Building in 1922 signaled that Loyola University was ready to move to the north-side campus and away from St. Ignatius College. It served as administrative offices, classrooms, library, and the residence of the Jesuit faculty. Affectionately known as "the Jes Res," it was demolished in 2008 to make way for the Information Commons.

The Administration Building served as the starting place for many of the events celebrated at Madonna della Strada Chapel. In this photograph, Knights of Columbus wait with Jesuit priests to join a Pan-American Day procession to the chapel. In 1989, the front steps and entrance to the Administration Building gained fame as the entrance to Taft Hospital in the movie *Flatliners*.

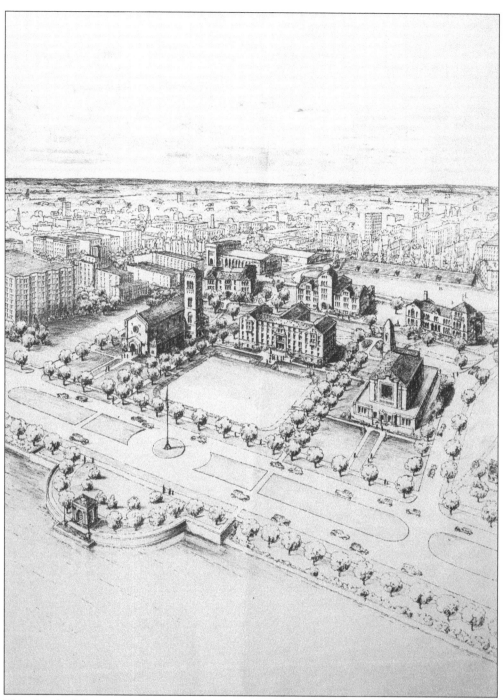

This sketch of the proposed campus plan from the 1930s still shows the anticipated extension of Lake Shore Drive north to Evanston. Half of the buildings in this sketch had been completed by the time it was done, namely Dumbach Hall, Cudahy Science Hall, the Administration Building, Cudahy Library, and Alumni Gym, along with the athletics field. Madonna della Strada Chapel and another classroom building had not been started. At far left, on the south end of Loyola's campus, is a building representing Mundelein College's skyscraper.

In 1922, the Loyola Jesuits received permission from the father general of the Society of Jesus to erect a gymnasium on the north-side campus. This sketch of the proposed gymnasium by architect Paul V. Hyland was drawn in 1923. Donations from alumni partially funded the construction, resulting in the name Alumni Gym. The gymnasium was demolished in 2011 to make way for Loyola's new student center.

Alumni Gym included an indoor running track, basketball courts, and a swimming pool in addition to offices for the athletics department. The swimming pool was the home of Loyola's intercollegiate swim and water polo teams during the 1970s and 1980s. The pool provided year-round exercise for Loyola students, staff, and faculty, as well as a safe place for local community residents to learn how to swim.

THE STUDENT ACTIVITIES BOARD OF LOYOLA UNIVERSITY

Proudly Presents

THE HOLLIES

DIRECT FROM LONDON, ENGLAND

ONE PERFORMANCE ONLY!

SUN. MARCH 10
7:00 P.M.

ALUMNI GYM
6525 N. SHERIDAN RD.

$3.00 per person - Tickets available at door

FOR INFORMATION CALL 274-3596

In addition to athletic competitions such as the National Catholic Interscholastic Basketball Tournament and intercollegiate basketball, Alumni Gym hosted other college events, often to the detriment of the basketball court. In the 1970s, the Student Activities Board, part of Loyola's Lake Shore Student Government Association, sponsored concerts for students in Alumni Gym, bringing in well-known groups like the Hollies.

ATTENTION!!
Chance of a Life Time
TO SEE

Johnny Weissmuller
Peter Weismuller
H. H. Kruger
Perry McGillivray
Sibyl Bauer
Minnie DeVry
Edna O'Connell
Ethel Leckie
Dorothy O'Brien

AND OTHER

Record Breaking Swimmers give an Exhibition and try for

NEW WORLD RECORDS in the

Loyola University Gymnasium Swimming Tank

Wednesday, Nov. 7, 8:30 p.m.

ADMISSION $1.00

Secure Tickets at Maguire's Drug Store or at Gym Office

ATTENDANCE LIMITED TO 600

Known as the best swim tank in Chicago when it opened, the Alumni Gym pool frequently hosted competitions and exhibitions featuring some of the best-known Chicago swimmers of the time. During the 1920s, one of the most frequently featured competitors was Johnny Weissmuller of Tarzan fame. These exhibitions often featured attempts at breaking world records.

Alumni Gym is best remembered as the home of the 1963 NCAA men's basketball champions. A team that did not shy away from challenging the norms of the day, coach George Ireland's 1963 Ramblers were the first college team to play four black starters, often against all-white teams. With 29 wins and only 2 losses for the 1962–1963 season, the Ramblers met the Cincinnati Bearcats in the championship game, winning in overtime 60-58. The victory went unrealized on Loyola's campus for several hours because, unlike today, college basketball was not televised live in the 1960s. The Loyola community back home had to wait for the tape-delayed broadcast of the game before celebrating the victory. The Loyola Ramblers remain the only men's college basketball team from Illinois to win the NCAA championship.

The athletic field on Loyola's Lake Shore Campus was the site of many different events. From the 1930s through the 1960s, one of the most common events was the annual "pushball" contest between the freshmen and sophomores. Freshmen were required to wear beanies during the first weeks of school to designate their status, a tradition enforced by the sophomores. After the Beanie Bounce dance, the freshmen and sophomores battled in a pushball contest to see if the freshmen would have to continue wearing the beanies. If the freshmen were victorious, they got rid of the beanies; if the sophomores won, they had to keep wearing them. The winning team took a victory lap around campus with their captain being pushed in a wheelbarrow and holding a small keg, while the losers had to jump into Lake Michigan.

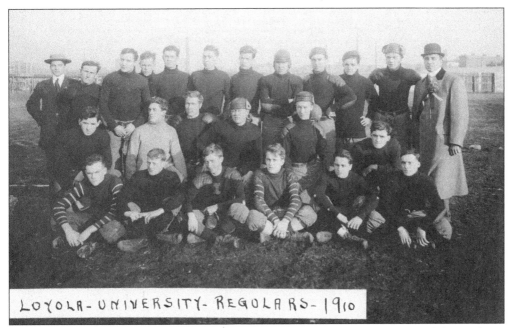

LOYOLA- UNIVERSITY- REGULARS- 1910

Football was the main sport played on the athletic field. Both the university and the academy teams used the field for practice and games. Occasionally, professional teams like the Green Bay Packers would use the field for practice, especially since it had lights for night games. Intercollegiate football, the sport that gave Loyola its "Ramblers" nickname (because the team had to take long train trips to play games), was eliminated in 1931. The official reason was lack of funds due to the Great Depression. When queried about the reasons for abandoning football, Robert M. Kelley, SJ, president from 1927 to 1933, stated that it was for financial, educational, and moral reasons. Although intercollegiate football is no longer around, football has carried on at Loyola as a club or intramural sport.

The Reserve Officers Training Corps (ROTC) has been part of Loyola since it was first established as the Students Army Training Corps in 1918. The original unit was disbanded in 1920 following World War I, but a new unit was established in 1948 and continues today. The ROTC used both the athletic field and the Broadway Armory for training and annual inspection reviews.

Built in 1930, the Elizabeth M. Cudahy Memorial Library was designed by famed Chicago architect Andrew N. Rebori. A gift to Loyola University by Edward A. Cudahy, founder of the Cudahy Packing Company, in honor of his wife, Elizabeth M. Cudahy, it was designed in the Classical/ Moderne-style with Art Deco decorations. Cudahy Library is the heart of Loyola's campus for studying and social interaction.

As with other buildings on the Lake Shore Campus, Cudahy Library was built with a door facing Lake Michigan in anticipation of the Lake Shore Drive expansion. The main door, however, was the south door by the sundial tower with its ornate Art Deco ironwork leading directly into the reading room. Today, this door is used for the commencement walk, graduation photographs, and other events.

Frederic Siedenburg, SJ, was the dean of the School of Sociology and regent of the Law School at the time that Cudahy Library was built. His estimate of 50 years before the library reached 250,000 volumes did not anticipate the printing boom following World War II; however, his prediction of a building in front of the Administration Building came true almost 80 years later when the Information Commons was built.

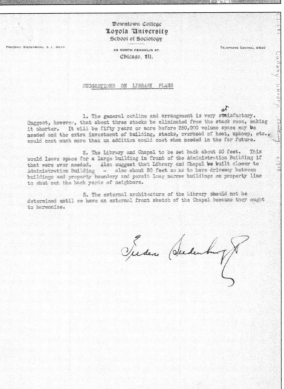

Born on May 24, 1882, feast day of Madonna della Strada, James J. Mertz, SJ, joined the Society of Jesus in 1900 and was ordained a priest in 1915. After teaching at St. Ignatius College for four years, he became one of the first Jesuit faculty members to transfer to the new Loyola University, where he served for 30 years as chair of the classical languages department. From 1924 to 1939, Mertz worked to raise more than $750,000 to build the Madonna della Strada Chapel on the Loyola University campus. The chapel opened in 1943 with only the exterior completed; however, it was still used for Mass. Following the completion of the chapel, Father Mertz could often be seen tending the flowers around it. He passed away in 1979 after 50 years of teaching at Loyola.

Construction of the Madonna della Strada Chapel in 1938 provided much-needed employment at the end of the Great Depression. Although labor was available for the work, construction was soon interrupted by the outbreak of World War II. Completion of the exterior of the chapel took five years due to the war's impact on materials and labor.

With construction finally complete in 1943, Mertz's "Poem in Stone" was ready to take its place at the center of campus life. Father Mertz returned to fundraising, this time with a campaign to complete the interior of the chapel. Primarily a private chapel for Loyola University, Madonna della Strada is considered a semi-public oratory, with members of the public welcome to attend Masses.

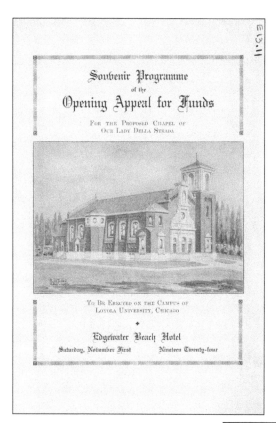

Souvenir Programme
of the
Opening Appeal for Funds

FOR THE PROPOSED CHAPEL OF
OUR LADY DELLA STRADA

TO BE ERECTED ON THE CAMPUS OF
LOYOLA UNIVERSITY, CHICAGO

✦

Edgewater Beach Hotel
Saturday, November First   Nineteen Twenty-four

Father Mertz was a master fundraiser who used a multi-prong attack. In addition to courting local Catholic residents, he arranged fundraising events at the Edgewater Beach Hotel, organized a student association to assist in soliciting funds, and, perhaps most memorable, arranged fundraising dances at the Aragon Ballroom. Except for six years, all of his fundraising work occurred during the Great Depression.

James J. Mertz, SJ, and Samuel K. Wilson, SJ, president of Loyola University from 1933 to 1942, look at a model of the proposed chapel. After rejecting several proposals, Father Mertz finally selected Andrew N. Rebori, the same architect who designed the Cudahy Library. Using the same Classical/Moderne style as the library for Madonna della Strada, Rebori created "bookends" for the great lawn in front of the Administration Building.

38

Although the interior of the chapel was not completed for another 10 years, it was still used for Masses and retreats. Memorials for Loyolans killed in World War II were held in the chapel, as were Masses for benefactors. The installation of officers for Loyola's Sodality chapter was also conducted in the chapel.

Madonna della Strada Chapel serves as the background for numerous events on campus. Baccalaureate Masses, such as the one pictured in this photograph, and honors convocations are common sights during May commencements. The Niehoff School of Nursing conducts its annual dedication to the profession ceremony at the chapel, and there are often choral and organ recitals scheduled throughout the year.

There is a small chapel in the crypt below the main chapel where two benefactors of Loyola, Ivan and Isabelle McKenna, are buried. Permission for the burials was granted in 1942 by Samuel K. Wilson, SJ, and Samuel Cardinal Stritch because Ivan McKenna had funded the construction of and Masses in the crypt. Following permission from Cardinal Stritch, the Chicago City Council passed an ordinance granting authority for the burials.

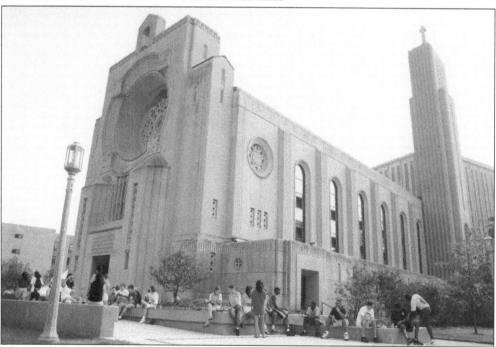

Over the years, Madonna della Strada Chapel has become a popular spot to sit by the lake alone or with friends, to study, talk, or just enjoy the sun and listen to the waves. It provides a place where people can commune with nature and enjoy a moment of peace during an otherwise busy day.

Loyola has both influenced the development of Sheridan Road and been influenced by it. Over the decades, Loyola buildings have replaced empty areas and older buildings on the street. In turn, Sheridan Road has constrained the direction that Loyola's main campus could grow. This photograph shows the empty corner at Sheridan Road and Loyola Avenue where the first dormitory, Campion Hall, would be built in 1955.

Numerous small businesses were situated south of the L tracks on Sheridan Road next to the Granada Theater, one of the grand movie palaces of Chicago. By the late 1980s, the Granada and other buildings were demolished and replaced by the Granada Center, an office building and dormitory, along with several apartment buildings.

Originally a garage for servicing cars, this building was converted into Loyola's Campus Center in 1950, moving student activities from Alumni Gym to their own space. Campus Center, also called the Loyola Union, included the Victory Room and the Rambler Room, a store, snack bar, and the university publications office. Campus Center was renamed Wilson Hall in honor of former Loyola president Samuel K. Wilson, SJ, in 1969.

Throughout the 1950s and 1960s, Loyola's Campus Center hosted student talent contests, variety shows, and Miss Loyola competitions. These talent contests and variety shows often included musical groups and comedy sketches and were an important part of building student camaraderie. Here, student nurses pose after performing the can-can at one such event in Wilson Hall's Rambler Room.

The era of big bands was still going strong in the 1950s and early 1960s. Locally and nationally known big bands and jazz bands often performed for dances and other events at the campus center. Among the bands to perform at Loyola during the 1950s were the Richard Maltby Band, the Bob Scobey Band, and the Dave Black Band.

Dances at the Loyola Union ranged from formal events to the more casual and were sponsored by different student organizations. The one in this photograph by Thomas J. Dyba, the 1953 Harvest Hop Square Dance, was sponsored by the University Co-Ed Club, a student organization that brought male and female students together in social situations.

In the mid-1960s, Loyola began preparing for its centennial in 1970 by constructing several new buildings. Damen Hall, a 10-story academic classroom and laboratory building, named for Loyola founder Arnold Damen, SJ, was built in 1966. Designed in the Brutalist architecture style, it was vastly different from previous campus buildings. Damen Hall was demolished in 2010 and replaced by a building resembling Dumbach and Cudahy Science Halls.

The campus quad formed by Damen Hall, Cudahy Science Hall, Dumbach Hall, Madonna della Strada Chapel, the Administration Building, and Cudahy Library often served as a gathering area for important events. In May 1970, faculty and students congregated in this area as Loyola and Mundelein participated in the nationwide student strike following the Kent State shootings. Mass was said by Jesuit priests in front of Damen Hall.

Completed in 1968, the James J. Mertz, SJ, complex was another departure from the original Mission-style buildings on campus. Named for the Jesuit responsible for the construction of Madonna della Strada Chapel, the complex included a 19-story dormitory, Centennial Forum Student Union, which replaced the Wilson Hall campus center, and Mullady Theater.

Named for School of Law alumnus Thomas U. Flanner III, who was an advocate of private education, Flanner Science Hall opened for classes in 1976. Built because of the need for a dedicated chemistry building, Flanner Hall was constructed with specialized laboratories to enable teaching and research in the field.

When Loyola decided to locate the humanities departments together, it was recognized that a new building was needed. The result was the Edward Crown Center for the Humanities, which opened in 1984. Named for a 1929 graduate of Loyola's medical school, the building was constructed to facilitate an interdisciplinary approach to teaching and research in the humanities.

After 72 years in Alumni Gym, Loyola basketball opened the 1996–1997 season in the new Joseph L. Gentile Center. Named for a Loyola alumnus from the class of 1948, Gentile Center seats 5,000 for basketball and volleyball. Alumni Gym continued to be used for practice until it was demolished in 2011.

Dedicated in 1982 to provide students, staff, and faculty with facilities to engage in recreational athletics, the George Halas Jr. Sports Center provides state-of-the-art facilities for basketball, volleyball, swimming, and numerous other recreational activities. The building was named in honor of George "Mugs" Halas, College of Commerce class of 1949, and son of George S. Halas.

Attending the 1982 dedication on behalf of NFL Charities, which contributed $200,000 to the construction of the Halas Sports Center, was NFL commissioner Pete Rozelle (left). Here, he joins George S. Halas (center), founder of the Chicago Bears and the National Football League, in receiving the key to the building from John Reinke, SJ.

Discussion about building a dormitory for the Lake Shore Campus began as early as 1924, although the father general of the Society of Jesus denied permission at the time. It was not until 1955 that the first dormitory was built, the Loyola University Residence Hall for Men, initiating Loyola's switch from a commuter school to a residential school. The dorm was later renamed Edmund Campion Hall in honor of St. Edmund Campion.

Stebler and Lewis Halls stood at the corner of Loyola and Winthrop Avenues on the north side of the Lake Shore Campus. Dedicated in 1960, Stebler Hall was the first women's residence on Lake Shore Campus. It was named for William J. Stebler, president of General American Transportation Corporation, and was the second women's dorm at Loyola following Delaware Hall on the Water Tower Campus.

In 1979, Loyola purchased the apartment building at 1000 Loyola Avenue to be used as undergraduate housing. Originally called Lake Front Hall, now called Santa Clara Hall, the building is on the north end of the campus next to Lake Michigan and across from the Crown Center for the Humanities.

The growing student population required an increase in dormitory space; thus, in 1991, Loyola opened the new living-learning center, a residence hall that included a new-style cafeteria and multi-purpose rooms for study and meetings. It was named in honor of William G. and Marilyn M. Simpson, who gifted $2 million for its construction.

Founded in 1930 by the Sisters of Charity of the Blessed Virgin Mary (BVM), Mundelein College was an all-girls school next to Lake Shore Campus. Originally an all-in-one college building (classrooms, offices, and living space for students and faculty in one building), Mundelein's campus expanded to include a dormitory, library, and student union. This aerial view shows Mundelein's campus in the 1930s.

The entrance to Mundelein College is guarded by two archangels: Uriel and Jophiel. Uriel, an angel of wisdom, is depicted holding the orb of the sun. Jophiel, an angel of wisdom, understanding, and judgment, is holding a book. Both archangels play key roles in Milton's *Paradise Lost*.

Sullivan Center was built in the 1960s as Mundelein College's library. The original building concept allowed for floors to be added as needed; however, due to concerns from other building owners in the area, this never happened. Following Mundelein's merger with Loyola, Sullivan Center became the Science Library and the first home of the Ann Ida Gannon, BVM, Center for Women and Leadership.

Built in 1908 for Albert Wheeler and his wife, Cassie, Wheeler House was one of the mansions on the north-side Gold Coast. Upon acquisition by Mundelein College, the house served first as the college library and later as the student union. Today, it is known as Piper Hall, for Mundelein alumna Virginia Piper and her husband, Kenneth, and is the home of the Gannon Center for Women and Leadership.

This aerial photograph shows Loyola's Lake Shore Campus in the 1950s. The academic buildings, library, gym, and chapel that create the core of the campus are visible, as is the Campus Towers apartment building. To the north of the library next to Campus Towers is the MacQueen house, which would be replaced 30 years later by the Crown Center.

This 1980 aerial photograph shows a different Lake Shore Campus than the one from the 1950s. The core campus buildings have been joined by Damen Hall, the Mertz complex, Halas Recreation Center, Flanner Hall, and Crown Center. Cudahy Library has received an addition, and Mundelein College has added a dormitory. Sidewalks and breakwalls had been added; however, there was still a beach between Loyola and Mundelein.

Three

Downtown College to Water Tower Campus

While the development of the north-side campus was underway, Loyola president Alexander J. Burrowes, SJ, was also overseeing the start of a downtown campus for the new university. This new campus was initiated by the advent of the first professional school, the School of Law, in 1908, which needed to be close to the practicing attorneys teaching the classes. The first location of the downtown campus was on the Ashland Block, now the Greyhound bus terminal. During the administration of John L. Mathery, SJ, president from 1912 to 1915, two more professional schools were established, the School of Sociology, and an evening school called University College, both in 1914. The School of Sociology, later renamed the School of Social Work, was established to provide Chicago teachers and other professionals with a chance to further their education on social issues of the time. From its establishment, the School of Sociology welcomed both men and women as students, a practice that was soon followed by the other professional schools. This led to an increase in students, and when two more schools opened—the College of Commerce in 1922 and the Graduate School in 1925—it became necessary to move the Downtown College to larger quarters on Franklin Street, where it remained until 1946.

Following World War II, philanthropist Frank J. Lewis purchased the former Illinois Women's Athletic Club building and presented it to Loyola University as a gift. Renamed Lewis Towers, this building remains the cornerstone of the Water Tower Campus today. The transformation of this campus into the home of Loyola's professional schools continued under the direction of presidents James T. Maguire, SJ, 1955–970, and Raymond C. Baumhart, SJ, 1970–1993, with the acquisition and construction of buildings, including the University Center, Siedenburg Hall, Maguire Hall, and the 25 East Pearson building (now Corboy Law Center). Following this expansion, further development of the Water Tower Campus would wait until the 21st century.

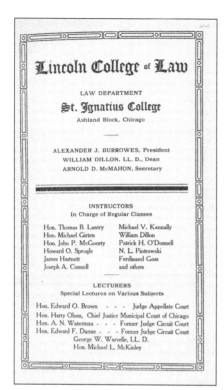

Lincoln College of Law

LAW DEPARTMENT

St. Ignatius College

Ashland Block, Chicago

ALEXANDER J. BURROWES, President
WILLIAM DILLON, LL. D., Dean
ARNOLD D. McMAHON, Secretary

INSTRUCTORS
In Charge of Regular Classes

Hon. Thomas B. Lantry	Michael V. Kannally
Hon. Michael Girten	William Dillon
Hon. John P. McGoorty	Patrick H. O'Donnell
Howard O. Sprogle	N. L. Piotrowski
James Hartnett	Ferdinand Goss
Joseph A. Connell	and others

LECTURERS
Special Lectures on Various Subjects

Hon. Edward O. Brown - - - Judge Appellate Court
Hon. Harry Olson, Chief Justice Municipal Court of Chicago
Hon. A. N. Waterman - - - Former Judge Circuit Court
Hon. Edward F. Dunne - - - Former Judge Circuit Court
George W. Warvelle, LL. D.
Hon. Michael L. McKinley

In 1906, Henry J. Dumbach, SJ, president of Loyola, received a letter from five prominent Catholic lawyers in Chicago requesting that St. Ignatius College open a law department. Initially named the Lincoln College of Law, William Dillon, one of the signers of the letter, became the first dean of the school. Tuition was $75 per year, and upon completion of the course, students received a bachelor of laws degree.

This 1924 photograph shows Florence McIntosh, secretary for the Law School, and an unidentified faculty member in the administrative offices of the Law School at Ashland Block. McIntosh eventually served as the secretary of the Graduate School in addition to the Law School as more professional schools were established at Loyola.

By 1926, the professional schools had outgrown their original quarters on the Ashland Block. Robert M. Kelley, SJ, Loyola president from 1927 to 1933, sought new quarters where the programs could expand, finally purchasing the 20–28 North Franklin Street building, former home of the Thompson-Ehlers Leather Co., in the Hearst Square Block.

Prior to opening, the 20–28 North Franklin Street building was remodeled by Loyola at a cost of $20,000 to provide offices, classrooms, and library space for the professional schools. Now officially called the Downtown College, the new building opened February 1, 1927. At first, the street level was occupied by shops, but eventually the schools expanded to the ground floor as the programs grew.

As regent of the Law School, Frederic Siedenburg, SJ, opened evening and weekend classes to women seeking law degrees. This photograph shows the first women to graduate from Loyola with a law degree. Seated are Clara Walsh Morris (left, class of 1927) and Marion Bremner (1926), while behind them is Mary G. Kelly (1927).

Beginning as the Loyola University Lecture Bureau, the School of Sociology originally offered study classes to help social workers, schoolteachers, and others interested in social work prepare for civil service examinations. The school also gave courses in civics and social economy as preparation for social and charity work of any kind. Tuition was $20 per term.

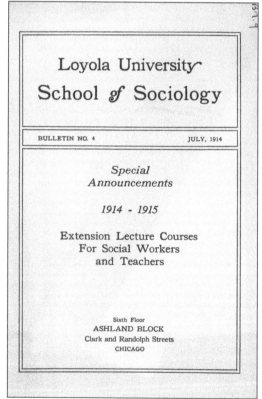

Loyola University
School of Sociology

BULLETIN NO. 4   JULY, 1914

Special
Announcements

1914 - 1915

Extension Lecture Courses
For Social Workers
and Teachers

Sixth Floor
ASHLAND BLOCK
Clark and Randolph Streets
CHICAGO

During his 21 years at Loyola University, Frederic Siedenburg, SJ, created an enduring legacy that still influences Loyola today. Siedenburg established the School of Sociology in 1914, the College of Commerce in 1924, the downtown branch of the College of Arts and Sciences and the Home Study Division in 1921, and reorganized the School of Law in 1921. He remained the Law School's regent and dean of the Downtown College until his reassignment to the University of Detroit in 1932. Among Siedenburg's many accomplishments were the creation of evening classes and part-time study and the admission of women to Loyola University. Here, he hands a diploma to a graduate in the 1920s.

Loyola's College of Commerce, first called the School of Commerce, opened in 1924 with evening classes. The school was the fourth professional school to enroll both men and women, following medicine, sociology, and law. Tuition in 1926 was $20 per subject per semester. Accounting and business law were $25 per semester.

After 17 years at the Ashland Block offices and almost 20 years at the Franklin Street building, a new location was needed once again to house the growing Downtown College. The search for a new location landed Loyola right next to Chicago's historic water tower, which would eventually give the new campus its name: the Water Tower Campus.

In 1946, philanthropist Frank J. Lewis presented Loyola University with the 17-story building at the corner of Pearson Street and East Tower Court. Known as Tower Court Building, it was renamed Lewis Towers and became the home of the Downtown College. In this photograph, James T. Hussey, SJ (left), president of Loyola from 1945 to 1955, and Frank J. Lewis stand outside the building entrance.

Built for the Illinois Women's Athletic Club in 1926 at a cost of $4 million, Tower Court had a pool, bowling alley, and gymnasium in addition to offices and lodging. The US Naval Reserve Midshipmen's School used the building from 1942 to 1945, training officers and providing cover for the operations of a US Army counter-espionage unit. Fall of 1946 saw 2,000 students arrive at Loyola's new downtown campus.

When Loyola received the Tower Court building, seven floors were reserved for the Illinois Catholic Women's Club, headed by Julia Deal Lewis. In 1963, Loyola students, staff, and faculty protested outside the building upon learning that the club was not allowing African Americans to use the pool. Loyola supported the right of individuals to protest but requested that the charitable work done by Lewis and her club be remembered.

Loyola's first AM radio station, WLUC, began broadcasting in the fall of 1967 in the student union at Lake Shore Campus. Soon after, WLT, a closed-circuit station run by the communication arts department, was on the air at Lewis Towers. WLUC and WLT were eventually phased out in favor of a new FM station, WLUW 88.7. Here, faculty mentor Dr. Sam Danna poses with the student staff of WLT.

Loyola University's Residence for Women, later renamed Delaware Hall, was acquired in 1956, the year after the opening of the Residence for Men on the Lake Shore Campus. The women's residence was two blocks from Lewis Towers and was formerly a nurse's home for Passavant Memorial Hospital. Room and board cost $760 per year for the 60 women in residence.

Loyola's president's office and other administrative offices were once located in this building at 840 North Wabash Avenue, north of Pearson Street. The building was eventually demolished and turned into a parking lot, which was replaced in turn by Baumhart Hall, Loyola's dormitory on the Water Tower Campus.

As president of Loyola from 1955 to 1970, James F. Maguire, SJ, oversaw the extensive growth and development of the Water Tower Campus. On April 26, 1961, he spoke at the ground breaking for the University Center, a five-story, $2.6 million building that included both academic spaces and gathering spaces for students and faculty.

Dedicated on September 22, 1962, and demolished in 2003, University Center, later renamed Marquette Center, was constructed to allow for the addition of five floors as needed for future expansion. The most notable exterior element of the building was the sky bridge that connected it to Lewis Towers. Albert Cardinal Meyer, archbishop of Chicago, presided over the blessing of the building.

This photograph showing the construction of the sky bridge between University Center and Lewis Towers also shows what Rush Street looked like in the early 1960s. Visible just north of Loyola's campus is the Archbishop Quigley Preparatory Seminary, run by the Archdiocese of Chicago and closed in 2007. The street past Quigley Seminary is remarkable for its lack of high rises, unlike the same area today.

The view south on Rush Street from Loyola's campus was vastly different in the 1960s than it is today. The lack of high rises allowed pedestrians to see the InterContinental Hotel, the Chicago Tribune Tower, and the Wrigley Building. Close to Marquette Center is a pub that became one of the hangouts for students, especially law students.

The *Spirit of Jesuit Higher Education* was a mosaic mural in the Georgetown room of the Marquette Center. Created by Melville P. Steinfels, a noted designer of liturgical art, this mosaic served as the backdrop for many events at the Water Tower Campus, including speakers and press conferences. It measured 34 feet and was made of ceramic tiles. The field was ecru,

buckskin, adobe, and topaz, while the design was in teal, sapphire, apricot, and citrine, and the figures were in assorted contrasting colors. The inscription on the mosaic was in Hebrew, Greek, and Latin, and translated to "Fear of the Lord is the Beginning of Wisdom." The mosaic was not relocated when Marquette Center was demolished in 2003.

Flapjaws Saloon became as much a part of the Water Tower Campus as Lewis Towers. Across from Loyola's campus on Pearson Street, generations of Loyola students attending classes at the Water Tower Campus congregated at Flapjaws for meals and social life. The building pictured here was demolished in 2005 to make way for Baumhart Hall, which included a space for Flapjaws on the ground floor.

After 50 years of sharing buildings with other professional schools, in 1958, the School of Law moved into its own building at 41 East Pearson Street. Law school alumni helped to raise $250,000 toward the $600,000 mortgage. Following the Law School's move to Maguire Hall in 1980, the School of Social Work moved into 41 East Pearson Street and renamed it Siedenburg Hall. The building was demolished in 2003.

Costing $4.5 million and specifically designed to accommodate the needs of the School of Law, the James F. Maguire, SJ, Hall was the fifth building to house the school and third building to do so on the Water Tower Campus. The 61,465-square-foot building housed classrooms, a courtroom for mock trial practice and competitions, and an auditorium.

Raymond C. Baumhart, SJ; Loyola president James F. Maguire, SJ; and Chicago mayor Michael A. Bilandic use jackhammers at the ground breaking of Maguire Hall in 1978. Maguire Hall was dedicated on May 27, 1980, with an invocation by James F. Maguire, SJ, former Loyola president and chancellor emeritus and the building's namesake, followed by a dedication address by Illinois governor James R. Thompson.

Raymond C. Baumhart, SJ, Loyola president (left), and Charles W. Murdoch, Loyola Law alumnus and dean of the Law School from 1975 to 1983, join other dignitaries in signing a beam for the topping-out ceremony of Maguire Hall. Topping out is when the last beam is placed atop a structure during construction.

The $36 million, 16-story building known as 25 East Pearson Street opened in July 1994 as the home of the School of Business Administration. Built on what was previously a parking lot, 25 East Pearson Street provides 310,000 square feet of academic space for graduate and undergraduate classes as well as Lewis Library, the library for the Water Tower Campus, and the School of Law library.

Four

CREATING A

MEDICAL CAMPUS

During Henry J. Dumbach, SJ's tenure as president, the St. Ignatius College consulters decided that Chicago needed a religiously oriented medical school. Creation of the school began under Alexander J. Burrowes, SJ, Loyola president from 1908 to 1912, with the affiliation of the Illinois Medical College, Reliance Medical College, and the Bennett Medical College in 1910, followed by the complete merger of these schools with Loyola in 1915, establishing the Loyola Medical Department, precursor to the School of Medicine. Following the acquisition of the Chicago College of Medicine and Surgery in 1917, Loyola finally had a home for its new school, where it would stay for the next 50 years.

In the 1920s, the Chicago College of Dental Surgery, founded in 1883, desired to affiliate with an established university to raise the standards of its dental education. Through the efforts of Dr. J.P. Harper, an alumnus and faculty member of the Chicago College of Dental Surgery, and Loyola's president William H. Agnew, SJ, a merger was achieved in late 1923, establishing the Loyola University School of Dentistry. Following a proud history of 110 years of education and innovation, the school was closed in 1993 due to declining enrollment.

The Loyola University School of Nursing was established in 1935 when five Chicago-area hospital schools—St. Bernard, St. Anne, St. Elizabeth, Oak Park, and Columbus—merged with Loyola University after two decades of affiliation. Sr. Helen Jarrell was appointed the first directress, later dean, of the new School of Nursing. In 1980, the School of Nursing was renamed the Marcella Niehoff School of Nursing in recognition of a generous gift from Marcella Niehoff, a local businesswoman.

In 1965, the Stritch School of Medicine, named in honor of Samuel Cardinal Stritch in 1948, broke ground on a new medical center in Maywood. The medical school moved to the Health Sciences Campus in 1967, followed by the Schools of Dentistry and Nursing in 1969. The Health Sciences Campus remains the home of the Stritch School of Medicine, the Niehoff School of Nursing, and the Loyola Medical Center today.

In the early 1900s, medical education was carried out largely by private institutions outside of universities and lacked consistent standards of education. Loyola University determined to create a medical school in Chicago that reflected its Jesuit values. It affiliated with independent medical colleges around the city, beginning with Illinois Medical College in 1909.

Bennett Medical College affiliated with Loyola in 1910 and later came under full control of the university in 1915. This course schedule from 1912 for students in their junior year described the weekly schedule of study. The week ran Monday to Saturday and included courses in surgery, anatomy, therapeutics, pathology, medicine, rhinology, and pediatrics.

Bennett Medical College

...OF CHICAGO...

MEDICAL DEPARTMENT
OF LOYOLA UNIVERSITY

JUNIOR SCHEDULE
FIRST SEMESTER
Sept. 26th, 1911 to Jan. 25th, 1912

Classes such as this one at Bennett Medical College in 1913 participated in hands-on study in their anatomy courses. This type of anatomical study is still present in medical schools today. Women enrolled in Bennett Medical College before and after its affiliation with Loyola and participated in all the same classes as male students, as witnessed by the female student in this photograph.

The Loyola University School of Medicine was established in 1915, when the Bennett Medical College came under full control of Loyola, and the medical department became a separate school within the university. The banquet celebration for the class of 1916 was at the historic La Salle Hotel at the corner of La Salle and Madison Streets in the Chicago Loop.

In 1917, Loyola purchased the Chicago College of Medicine and Surgery at 706 South Wolcott Avenue (then Lincoln Street). Students began clinical rotations that year at nearby area hospitals. Loyola University School of Medicine classes formally began in this building in 1918. In 1919, Dr. Bertha Van Hoosen became the first woman appointed chairperson and professor of obstetrics at the school.

George Cardinal Mundelein, archbishop of Chicago, donated $20,000 from diocesan parish collections to support the fledgling Loyola School of Medicine. In 1921 and 1924, the old Chicago College of Medicine and Surgery building was extensively remodeled for the use of the Loyola School of Medicine. This building was home to the School of Medicine for nearly 50 years before relocating to the Health Sciences Campus in Maywood in 1967.

Medical education in Loyola's early years, as with most other American medical schools, was structured as a six-year program. Students attended two years of undergraduate college and then advanced to medical school. Similar to the modern-day curriculum, the last two years of training consisted of clinical rotations at nearby hospitals.

The obstacle Loyola faced from the late 1920s to the late 1940s was funding. The cost of medical education was far greater than the tuition received. The Great Depression and the enrollment decline due to World War II were keenly felt in the medical school. Financial support from Samuel Cardinal Stritch and community members such as Frank and Julia Deal Lewis ensured the survival of the school.

In 1943, the Loyola University medical unit of the US Army, General Hospital Unit No. 108, was reactivated for World War II service and was staffed with Loyola-trained nurses and doctors. Here, Loyola president Samuel Knox Wilson, SJ, poses with Col. George T. Jordan, director of the 108th Medical Unit (left) and Lt. Col. Francis Fitts, director of all US Army hospitals.

A. C. 25. - CLICHY. — L'Hôpital Beaujon

The Loyola medical unit was reported to be one of the largest groups of its kind ever formed. The 108th moved into the Hospital Beaujon in Clichy, France, just two miles outside of Paris. Fifteen boxcars were needed to carry all the beds, linens, medicines, and operating equipment to Clichy. While in residence at the Beaujon, the unit served over 60,000 patients.

The history of the 108th traces to World War I, when it was organized toward the end of the war. It was demobilized without ever serving overseas. During World War II, the unit was reactivated and staffed by 60 doctors and 115 nurses trained by Loyola, along with 800 enlisted men. Annual reports on the units' duties and activities were produced by the commander.

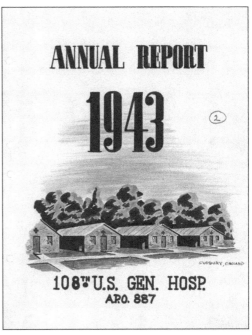

ANNUAL REPORT 1943

108ᵀᴴ U.S. GEN. HOSP.
A.P.O. 887

ANNUAL REPORT 1944

108ᵀᴴ U.S. GEN. HOSP.
A.P.O. 887

Members of General Hospital Unit No. 108 were permitted to wear their own badge, a privilege not granted to other medical units. The insignia displayed a roaring lion, in Loyola's official colors of maroon and gold, with the motto "Pro Deo et Patria" (for God and Country). Loyola medical school professor Col. George T. Jordan reactivated the unit following the attack on Pearl Harbor.

On April 15, 1948, Loyola's board of trustees unanimously approved a resolution to name the Loyola School of Medicine the Stritch School of Medicine in honor of Samuel Cardinal Stritch, archbishop of Chicago, as an acknowledgment of the prominent role he played in ensuring the survival of the school through a number of fundraising efforts such as the annual Cardinal's Dinner.

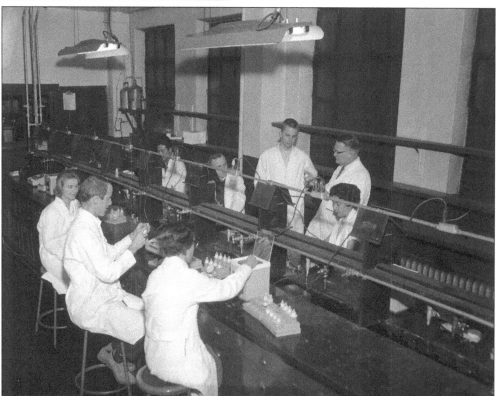

Medical education at Loyola was heavily influenced by the landmark 1910 Flexner Report, which lambasted Chicago area medical schools, calling their poor standards and weak curricula "a plague spot of the country." Loyola was one of the first medical schools to follow the Flexner report recommendations and even increased the requirement for formal training in the basic sciences for students.

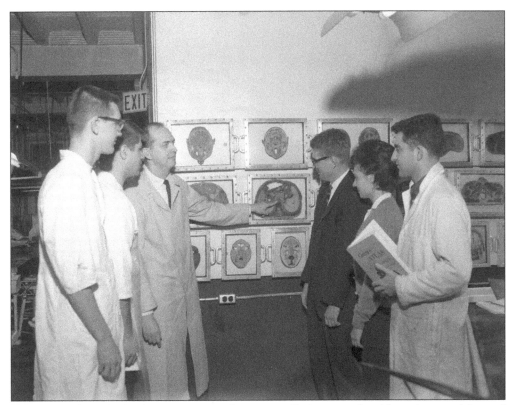

Standards of medical education at Loyola continually increased, with updates to labs and classrooms. By 1930, students were doing clinical rotations at the nationally recognized Cook County Hospital, which offered an excellent faculty and patient population. In 1955, James F. Maguire, SJ, a key medical school supporter, became president of Loyola University, and the push to expand the medical school began.

In 1961, Loyola purchased a 62-acre parcel from the Hines Veterans Administration Hospital and site of the former Old Speedway Race Track, to develop an extensive new medical center. Hines Hospital was established following World War I, when veterans returning home required access to medical care at a hospital. Construction on what was popularly known as the "Speedway Hospital" for veterans began in 1918.

View of the Old Speedway Race Track, with Grandstand on Whose Foundation Main Hospital Was Erected

The Hines Veterans Administration Hospital contained a main infirmary building that was 2,040 feet long, 50 feet wide, and four stories high. Half of the building was used as an 864-bed hospital, with the other half serving as quarters for hospital personnel. This aerial photograph shows the extensive Hines campus.

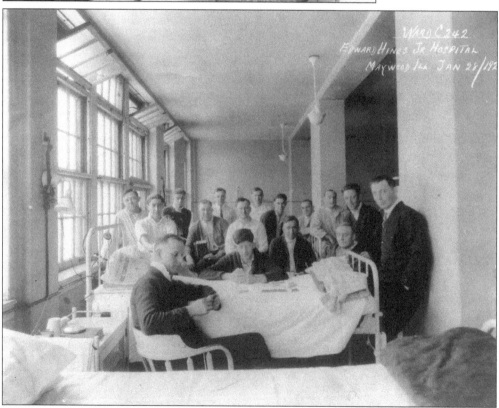

The Hines Hospital was named for Edward Hines Jr., the son of millionaire Edward Hines, who donated a substantial sum for the construction of the hospital in honor of his son who had died in service during World War I. Pictured here are veterans receiving treatment in Hines Hospital Ward C242 in January 1925.

Construction began on the new medical center in 1965. By 1967, the Stritch School of Medicine had moved to the facility in Maywood, and by 1969, the School of Nursing and School of Dentistry also moved to what eventually became known as the Health Sciences Campus. The medical center included a hospital, motel for patient families, student residences, and an educational center.

In 1969, a new 451-bed teaching hospital on the Maywood campus opened. Later named for Foster G. McGaw, a businessman and veteran who gave $7 million to fund its construction, the Foster G. McGaw Hospital was dedicated in November 1972. From left to right are McGaw, executive vice president Father Baumhart, SJ, and Loyola president Father Maguire, SJ, at the dedication.

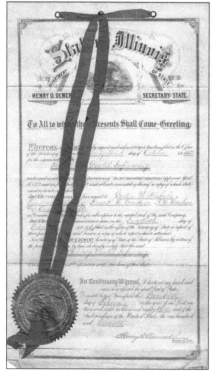

The beam signing for the Leischner Medical Education Building construction occurred in 1996. The building was named for Dr. Ralph Leischner, who was instrumental in designing and implementing the new medical education curriculum at Stritch. From left to right are Al Gorman; Dr. Frank Banich, class of 1957; Victor Heckler; Dr. Dan Winship; Loyola president John Piderit, SJ; Matt Bosse, class of 1999; Dr. Anthony Barbato, class of 1970; and Dr. Ralph Leischner, class of 1968.

The city of Chicago was just 50 years old when the Chicago Dental Infirmary opened its doors. Established in 1883, as shown on this act of incorporation by the State of Illinois, the Chicago Dental Infirmary was the city's first dental school thanks to the efforts of Dr. Truman W. Brophy.

The Chicago Dental Infirmary was re-chartered in 1884 as the Chicago College of Dental Surgery. In the summer of 1893, the college moved to the southeast corner of Harrison and Wood Streets. This location was chosen due to its proximity to other prominent medical colleges and hospitals, as well as the elevated railway lines.

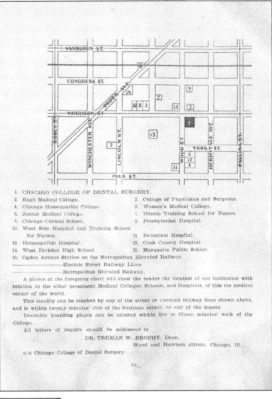

In the early 1920s, as part of an effort to raise the standard of dental education, the Chicago College of Dental Surgery affiliated with Loyola University. In 1923, Dr. William H.G. Logan (left), treasurer of the Chicago College of Dental Surgery, and Loyola president William H. Agnew, SJ, shake hands as the college became the Dental Department of Loyola University.

The Harrison Street building transitioned from the Chicago College of Dental Surgery to the Dental Department of Loyola University in 1923. The building was renovated in 1937 to provide a new and modern clinic and research laboratory. The dental department was renamed the Loyola University School of Dentistry in 1950 and remained in the Harrison building until relocating to the Health Sciences Campus in 1969.

The main entrance to the Harrison Street building welcomed students to a rigorous dental education. Seeking to always improve educational standards, the School of Dentistry housed a museum of rare dental instruments on the third floor and hired top faculty members who were well published and making significant contributions to dentistry.

THE MAIN ENTRANCE.

The School of Dentistry assured that students were given instruction by well-regarded professionals with access to modern laboratories and equipment. In 1957, Dr. William P. Schoen, dean from 1956 to 1973, oversaw the repurposing of a chemistry lab into an orthodontic research laboratory and a prosthetics processing laboratory and the purchase of cephalometric radiography equipment for better instruction and preparedness of students.

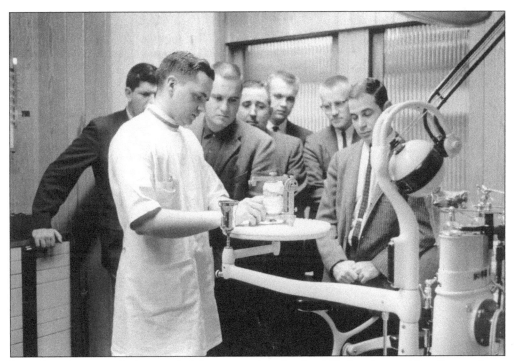

Dental students regularly attended demonstrations by the skilled and expert faculty members, as pictured here, and benefited from the teaching relationship with the 2,700-bed Cook County Hospital, directly across the street from the Harrison building. Senior dental students were required to attend diagnostic and surgical clinics at the hospital.

Hands-on experience in labs to prepare students to be capable dentists serving the public has always been a cornerstone of the school's dental education. In the early days of dentistry, most dental instruments were hand-wrought and hand-sharpened. Cavities were prepared by hand until powered drills were introduced to the profession.

The Dental School was also the first institution of its kind to introduce and use, for the benefit of its students, apparatuses for the cultivation of bacteria. This innovation in dental education allowed students to study the agents that were actively causing dental maladies and the preventative measures that could be taken.

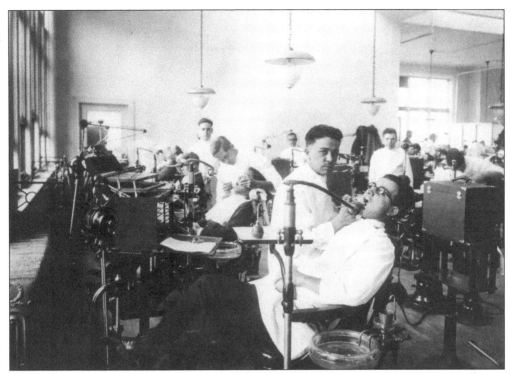

The School of Dentistry offered dental services to members of the community, which allowed students to obtain real-world practice. The Dental Clinic provided services to nearly 300 community members daily, an average of about 70,000 per year. In addition to the Dental Clinic, students often practiced techniques on their classmates, as seen in this photograph.

In addition to lab and clinical work, lectures were also a part of the dental education at Loyola. Lecture halls in the Harrison building had a seating capacity of 143 students and were equipped with four television monitors so students could have close-up views of instruction on techniques and procedures.

Loyola's School of Dentistry constantly sought to be an innovator in dental education, and in 1954, Loyola became the first dental school to acquire a closed-circuit teaching television system. Students typically crowded around one dental chair to observe the techniques of their professors, which did not permit adequate observation. A closed-circuit television system allowed for a larger number of students to observe the procedures and techniques.

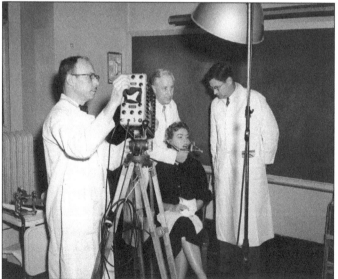

The Education Television Department, created after the purchase of the closed-circuit television system, included a studio completely equipped with operating facilities similar to those found in the clinical areas. From this studio, an instructor could demonstrate techniques and procedures with a clear view for an entire lecture hall of students.

This innovation in dental education allowed the School of Dentistry to admit more students, as they were no longer constrained by how many students could stand around a professor to view a procedure or technique. Any demonstration, technique, or clinical procedure from anywhere in the dental school building could be broadcast to any classroom with a clear and unobstructed view.

In the spring of 1958, the School of Dentistry celebrated its diamond jubilee. The celebration included a banquet marking the 75th anniversary and the presentation of several awards. The college choir, comprised of dental students, provided entertainment for the banquet under a banner celebrating the past deans of the School of Dentistry.

As the Stritch School of Medicine moved to the new medical center campus in Maywood, ground was broken on the campus for a new dental school in 1967. The School of Dentistry moved to Maywood in 1969. A ribbon-cutting ceremony was held on August 18, 1969, with Dr. William P. Schoen, dean of the School of Dentistry, cutting the ribbon next to executive vice president Raymond C. Baumhart, SJ.

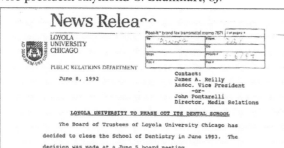

Loyola University announced in June 1992 that the School of Dentistry would close in June 1993. Declining enrollment, rising costs for dental education, and the need for fewer dentists to serve the population were the reasons cited for the closure. The School of Dentistry left a legacy of innovative dental education and more than 7,000 alumni.

Nursing education at Loyola started in 1916 with the affiliation of the St. Bernard School of Nursing at St. Bernard Hospital on the south side of Chicago. The original nursing program was comprised of a series of affiliations with hospital schools throughout the city, specifically St. Bernard, St. Anne, St. Elizabeth, Oak Park, and Columbus. The hospital schools of St. Francis in Evanston, Mercy Hospital, and John B. Murphy affiliated with Loyola later. In 1935, the Loyola University Board of Trustees established the School of Nursing by forming a governing board with the directors of the five original hospital schools, with St. Francis Hospital School joining in 1936. The School of Nursing consisted of six units, with each hospital school designated as a unit. Students enrolled in these hospital schools were considered students of Loyola University.

Terrence H. Ahearn, SJ, regent of Loyola's Medical School, recommended that Sr. Helen Jarrell, Religious Hospitallers of St. Joseph (RHSJ), director of nursing at St. Bernard Hospital, be appointed to lead the School of Nursing. Sister Jarrell is the sister at center in this 1927 St. Bernard's graduation photograph. (Photograph from St. Bernard School of Nursing Fonds, Loyola University Archives and Special Collections. Used with permission of the Religious Hospitallers of St. Joseph, Kingston, Ontario.)

Sr. Helen Jarrell, a member of the RHSJ, was appointed as the first directress and later dean of the Loyola School of Nursing in 1935. Her tenure as dean, which lasted until 1947, included the creation of a public health nursing program, securing the nurses needed for Loyola's 108th General Hospital during World War II, and the creation of a bachelor of nursing curriculum at Loyola.

Gladys Kiniery, pictured pinning a nursing student, became the second dean of the School of Nursing in 1947. A Loyola alumna, she earned her bachelor's degree in nursing in 1936 and her master's degree in public health from the University of Michigan in 1940. Kiniery served as dean until 1966. Under her leadership, the school became the first fully accredited college of nursing in Illinois.

Guests of Eli Lilly and Company

GRADUATE NURSES
LOYOLA UNIVERSITY
DEPARTMENT OF PUBLIC HEALTH NURSING
CHICAGO, ILLINOIS

JUNE 10, 11, AND 12, 1953

BASS PHOTO CO.

In 1938, a public health nursing program was established at the School of Medicine, and in 1941, the program was accredited by the National Organization of Public Health Nursing. In 1948, the School of Nursing was reorganized, uniting the departments of nursing, nursing education, and public health nursing, allowing for an integrated bachelor of science in nursing degree.

Loyola's dedication to public health nursing and clinical experience for nursing students is seen in this photograph, as a Loyola student nurse stands outside the free chest x-ray bus for the Tuberculosis Institute of Chicago and Cook County at the intersection of Lincoln, Belmont, and Ashland Avenues in 1955. The Tuberculosis Institute of Chicago and Cook County was dedicated to reducing the number of tuberculosis cases in Chicago.

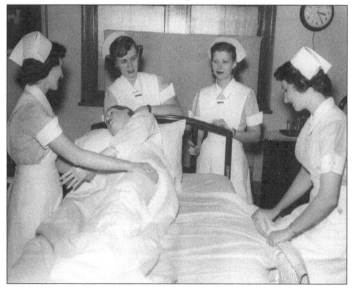

In 1960, the School of Nursing celebrated its silver anniversary with a three-day program featuring educational, social, and spiritual exercises. The Alpha Beta chapter of Sigma Theta Tau was established on the Loyola campus in 1965, making Loyola's School of Nursing the first collegiate nursing program in Illinois to have a chapter.

The pinning ceremony is a nursing tradition that welcomes newly graduated nurses into the profession. During the ceremony, each graduate takes the Nightingale Pledge, which will help guide them throughout their nursing career. The pinning ceremony is always held in the Madonna della Strada Chapel on the Lake Shore Campus.

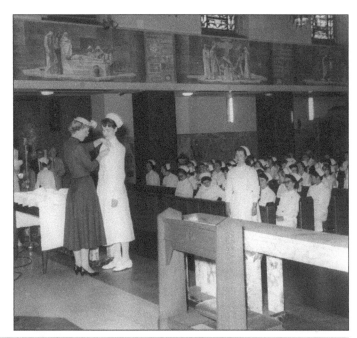

The School of Nursing has always enjoyed the enthusiastic support of the Chicago community. The Nursing Fund Team, tasked with raising funds for the school and spreading awareness about the nursing program, was comprised of alumnae and interested members of the community who held numerous fundraising events for the school.

Loyola nursing students Diane Annweiler (left) and Pamela Osborn stand in front of a poster to help promote anti-smoking in all communities. Harkening to Loyola's involvement with the Tuberculosis Institute of Chicago and Cook County, these nursing students were participating in the national public health campaign to get people to quit smoking.

In 1975, Dr. Julia Lane was named the sixth dean of the School of Nursing. During her 16-year tenure as dean, the School of Nursing grew from three to seven areas of specialization, began a doctoral program, and increased the number of students and faculty. Although she stepped down as dean in 1991, Lane continued to teach in the School of Nursing until her retirement in 1994.

Five years after Dr. Lane was named dean of the School of Nursing, Marcella Niehoff endowed the school with $3 million. The endowment was inspired by the high quality of nursing care the Niehoff family had received from the School of Nursing. In 1980, the school was renamed the Marcella Niehoff School of Nursing in honor of her generosity.

The Niehoff School of Nursing celebrated its golden jubilee in 1985. At this point, it was the largest nursing program in Illinois. The degree offerings included the traditional baccalaureate program, a baccalaureate completion program for RNs, three master's programs, and the beginnings of a doctoral program. By this time, the school had joined the medical and dental schools on the Maywood campus.

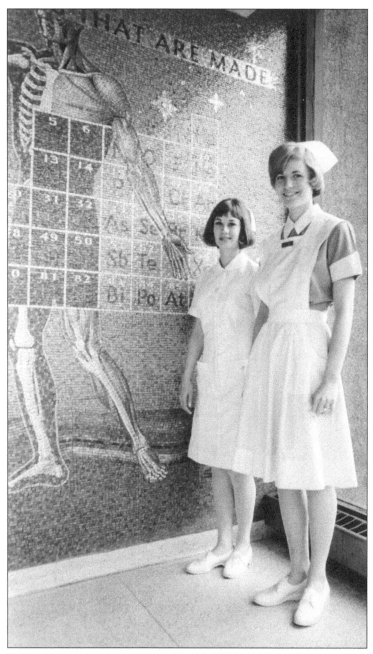

The efforts of Dean Kiniery in the mid-1960s resulted in a construction grant designating two floors of Damen Hall as the permanent home of the School of Nursing on the Lake Shore Campus. A mosaic by Melville Steinfels titled *Wonders of Creation* was unveiled in Loyola University's Damen Hall in 1966 and expresses God's infinite order and beauty as they become known through mathematics and science. In 2012, the mosaic was moved to the new Marcella Niehoff School of Nursing building on the Maywood campus. Artist David Lee Csicsko added sections to the mosaic, filling in former doorways, to accommodate its setting in the new building, which was dedicated on September 29, 2012.

Five

A CAMPUS IN
THE ETERNAL CITY

In 1962, John Felice, SJ, led the first group of Loyola students to Rome for a study abroad trip. A Jesuit from Malta, Felice had worked with the US Army during World War II. Following the war, he was assigned to Loyola University as a classical studies professor. Felice's dream was to establish a branch of Loyola's College of Arts and Sciences in Rome, where American students could study for a semester or a year and be exposed to European history and art. This dream led to Loyola establishing the first permanent study abroad program in Rome during the presidency of James F. Maguire, SJ.

The first study abroad semester occurred at the Casa Italiana Viaggi Internazionali Studenti (CIVIS). CIVIS was built for the 1960 Rome Olympics and was provided to Loyola by the Italian government. This campus served as the home of the Loyola study abroad program, the Rome Center for Liberal Arts, until 1966. Expanding student interest in the program and increased attendance required the program to find a larger location, and in 1966, it moved to its second site, the Villa Tre Colli on the Via de Cammillucia. The Villa Tre Colli location marked the beginning of the Rome Center's residency on the Monte Mario. Further student expansion led to another move in 1972 to the Villa Maria Theresa on the Via Trionfale, where the Rome Center remained until 1978, when it moved to what would become its permanent home on the Via Massimi. Today, the John Felice Rome Center welcomes Loyola students and students from other colleges and universities for a semester or year-long program.

John P. Felice, SJ, founder of the Rome Center, was born on the island of Malta in 1923. During World War II, he served as a British intelligence liaison officer and often interacted with American troops. This experience influenced his life's work of bridging cultural gaps and fostering education and tolerance. In 1946, he entered the Society of Jesus and was ordained in 1957. He eventually left the order to marry. Following his acceptance of an assistant professorship position on the theology faculty at Loyola University, Felice organized a European tour for faculty and graduate students. After the tour, Felice was invited to a lunch with the Italian president Giovanni Gronchi and American ambassador Clare Booth Luce. Conversation during that lunch led directly to the establishment of Loyola's Rome Center in 1962.

In 1961, John Felice, SJ, led a summer European trip for 65 faculty members and graduate students. This trip further strengthened his commitment to bridging cultural gaps through education and led to the meeting that sparked the creation of the Rome Center. Among the people on this tour was James J. Mertz, SJ. It was Mertz's first trip to Europe.

January 5, 1962, saw the arrival of the first students to study at the newly established Rome Center. Three faculty members traveled by ship with 92 students to Rome. The first building that housed the new study abroad program was CIVIS, provided by the Italian government.

CIVIS was shared with international students from other schools who were in Rome for study abroad programs. For the initial semester of Loyola's program, Dr. Michael Fink taught art history; Dr. George Szemler taught history; Fr. John L. McKenzie, SJ, taught classical studies; Rosemary Donatelli taught education; and Dr. Cecelia Bartoli taught Italian. Here, faculty members watch students on their way to class.

Following that first semester, 200 students applied for the full year of study to be offered during the 1962–1963 academic year, and 100 attended the program. Classes were held in five halls in the basement of the international house across from where the Loyola students were housed.

Ties between Loyola's Rome Center for the Liberal Arts and the Italian government were strong from the inception of the program. Not only did the Italian government provide the first building for the program, but Italian dignitaries often attended events at the Rome Center. In 1962, the first special convocation was held at the Rome Center welcoming dignitaries, including Giovanni Gronchi, former president of Italy. Students and faculty had a formal audience with Italian president Antonio Segni in 1962 at Quirinal Palace. In recognition of the relationship between Loyola and Italy, students and faculty of the Rome Center visited Piazza Venezia and laid a wreath at the Tomb of the Unknown Soldier.

During the winter break of 1962–1963, students and faculty from the Rome Center went on a Christmas tour of Greece, Turkey, Lebanon, Syria, Jordan, Israel, and the Holy Land. This was the start of what would become Rome Center's annual Middle East tour, part of Felice's philosophy of bridging cultural gaps by educating students about different cultures.

John Felice, SJ, stands in front of the Parthenon in Athens, Greece, with two women during one of the annual Middle East tours that he arranged. These tours exposed students and staff to a variety of cultures, thus expanding on the international education offered at the Rome Center.

Rome Center students took advantage of both the European orientation tours before they reached the Rome Center and the Middle East tours offered over the winter break to learn about and interact with different cultures. This group of students stands by the Acropolis in Athens, which was part of the tour.

In 1966, the Rome Center moved to its second location, the Villa Tre Colli, where it stayed until 1972. The villa was on 25 acres at the top of the Monte Mario. This new location expanded the facilities available to Loyola's Rome Center and allowed for the number of classes to increase.

The rooftop patio of the Villa Tre Colli was a popular place where students often gathered to relax, study, and plan trips around Italy or Europe. This vantage point allowed them to view the entirety of the villa's 25 acres while enjoying the Roman sunshine. Views like this reminded the students that they were not back home in the United States.

In November 1966, Rome Center students drove to Florence, Italy, by car in order to help in the aftermath of the infamous Florence Flood. Under the guidance of Fr. Pierre Riches, Rome Center students, such as the ones in this photograph, assisted Florentines in recovering from the disaster and rescuing some of the treasures of Florence.

The 10th year of the Rome Center's existence, 1972, began with another move, this time to the Clinica Maria Teresa, near the Villa Tre Colli. The gates of the new location opened onto a tree-lined drive that led to the building. Rome Center remained at this location until 1978.

The seven-story Clinica Maria Teresa, also called the Villa Maria Teresa, provided more classroom, office, study, and recreational space for the Rome Center. However, it housed almost 300 fewer students than the previous property. There were also six acres of woods and gardens that could be used for recreational purposes.

According to John Felice, SJ, the renovation of the new property continued right up to the arrival of the students for the 1972 fall semester. Soon after classes started, a new library of 40,000 volumes arrived, giving the Rome Center one of the largest libraries attached to a foreign study program in Rome.

The stairway of the Villa Maria Teresa was one of the highlights of the campus, offering students a place to study, gather, or just relax and enjoy the weather, and was often the designated meeting place for beginning trips. Here, students congregate as they get ready to depart on a trip to explore Rome.

Travel played a large part in Felice's philosophy of bridging cultural gaps. Rome Center students were encouraged to explore Rome and Europe individually or in groups as often as they could. Every other Friday was free of classes so that students could spend long weekends traveling around Italy and other countries.

Cathy Grady waits to catch the No. 67 bus that will take her into the center of Rome. Rome Center students took advantage of being in one of the most historic cities in the world and explored whenever they had a chance. Classes were often held in locations other than the classroom in order to connect students to what they were learning about.

In 1978, the Rome Center moved once again to its fourth and final location, Via Massimi on the Monte Mario. Loyola University purchased the property in 2006, finally bringing an end to the program's roaming and positioning it for future growth. In 2009, it was renamed the John Felice Rome Center.

One of the most popular spots at the John Felice Rome Center is the center courtyard. Surrounded by campus buildings, it provides a secure place for students to meet before or after classes as well as offering a spot for them to study, socialize, or engage in outdoor recreational activities.

Six

LOYOLA IN
THE 21ST CENTURY

Throughout its 150-year history, Loyola University Chicago has undergone many changes in its programs and physical locales. Now well established in its current locations, the advent of the 21st century has seen campus improvements and modernization of spaces to carry the university forward. On the Lake Shore Campus, Damen Hall, Alumni Gym, and the Jesuit Residence have been demolished and replaced with new buildings, and two quad areas have been created. On the Water Tower Campus, Marquette Center, Siedenburg Hall, and 840 North Wabash Avenue have been demolished and replaced with the Clare/School of Communications, Baumhart Hall, and the Schreiber Center. The John Felice Rome Center has a permanent campus on the Via Massimi with the purchase of its fourth site, and the Health Sciences Campus continues to expand research and care facilities through the construction of cutting-edge buildings. While this expansion has gone on at the existing campuses, three new campuses have joined the university—the Cuneo Mansion and Gardens campus in Vernon Hills, Illinois, the Retreat and Ecology Campus in Woodstock, Illinois, and the Vietnam Center in Ho Chi Minh City.

Loyola University Chicago's commitment to the Jesuit tradition of social justice and care for creation through local action that creates global impact can be seen in its dedication to environmental sustainability. New buildings on the Lake Shore, Water Tower, and Health Sciences Campuses adhere to the LEED guidelines for green and sustainable construction, and environmental studies degree programs have been expanded with the addition of the Institute of Environmental Sustainability. The belief in the dignity of every person is reflected in Loyola's dedication to the Deferred Action for Childhood Arrivals (DACA) students in the Stritch School of Medicine and other programs throughout the university. Loyola moves through the 21st century with its mission in mind: "We are Chicago's Jesuit, Catholic University—a diverse community seeking God in all things and working to expand knowledge in the service of humanity through learning, justice and faith."

In 2005, planning began for a new building adjoining the Cudahy Library on the Lake Shore Campus. Newly appointed dean of libraries Robert Seal was drawn to Loyola to lead the planning for the new Information Commons. A joint project with the university libraries and information technology services, the Information Commons is meant to reflect the "3C" philosophy of collaboration, connectivity, and community.

The Information Commons opened in 2008, with the architecture of the building demonstrating Loyola's commitment to sustainability and environmental awareness. It features Chicago's first double-skin facade for passive management of heat flow and ventilation, a green roof, and sensor-activated, mechanical blinds. The names of famous philosophers, theologians, and saints adorn the tops of the outer masonry walls, connecting it to Madonna della Stada Chapel and Cudahy Library.

Damen Hall on the Lake Shore Campus was demolished in 2010 and replaced with Cuneo Hall, which opened in 2012. Named for Loyola benefactors John and Herta Cuneo, the building returns to the original Mission-style aesthetic of neighboring Cudahy Science Hall and Dumbach Hall. A Gold-LEED certified building, it features a green roof, an in-slab radiant heating and cooling system, and an atrium that allows for natural stack-effect ventilation.

The Institute of Environmental Sustainability, a Gold-LEED building, opened in 2013 on the Lake Shore Campus and contains classrooms, research and teaching labs, a biodiesel lab, and an urban agricultural greenhouse, all connected to a residence hall. The completion of the institute created Kenmore Plaza, turning a city street into a pedestrian-only area.

As Loyola creates more degree programs focusing on environmental studies, the Institute of Environmental Sustainability offers students an opportunity to interact in a building designed to support sustainability. Three green roofs and a rain capture system collect water that is reused in the greenhouse operations. The building's geothermal system is the largest in Chicago.

Dr. Nancy Tuchman, dean of the Institute of Environmental Sustainability, supports students in acquiring the skills to become leaders in environmental research and policy. The Searle Biodiesel Lab is a student-run business providing biodiesel to the shuttle bus system and hand soap to the campus. An aquaponics system provides experience with fish farming and aquaponic agriculture, and the ecotoxicology research lab enables research on the role of containments in ecosystems.

112

In 2005, Loyola president Michael J. Garanzini, SJ, oversaw the renovation of the interior of the Madonna della Strada Chapel on the Lake Shore Campus. Artist Meltem Aktas renovated the fresco on the west wall and added gold leaf to the Stations of the Cross, both originally created by Melville Steinfels, and a new white marble baptismal font and marble floor were installed along with a new altar and ambo.

In 2015, four custom-made bells were hoisted to the top of the tower in the Madonna della Strada Chapel. The bronze bells were named Ignatius, after St. Ignatius of Loyola; Cecilia, after the couples married in the chapel; James, in memory of Fr. James J. Mertz, SJ; and Joseph, in honor of St. Joseph Pignatelli. The bells play "Madonna Quarters," composed by Steven Betancourt, Loyola's director of liturgical music.

As part of President Garazini's *reimagine* plan, the Arnold J. Damen, SJ, Student Center opened in 2013. Standing in the place of the demolished Alumni Gym, the Damen Student Center is a student union containing a food court, student lounges, religious spaces for faith groups, and offices for the Division of Student Development. The Student Center is named for Loyola's founder, Fr. Arnold J. Damen, SJ.

The Damen Student Center became the place for students to watch Loyola's men's basketball team during the 2018 NCAA tournament. Ireland's Pub, named for legendary Loyola coach George Ireland, was the preferred place for students to watch the games, but viewing eventually took over the entire first floor as the Ramblers advanced to the Final Four.

A new three-story home for Loyola's student athletes was opened in 2011 on the Lake Shore Campus, the Norville Center for Intercollegiate Athletics. Named for trustee and former Rambler basketball player Allan Norville (class of 1960), it features a strength and conditioning center, larger locker rooms, and sports medicine facility. Since opening, Norville Center has witnessed the men's volleyball team win back-to-back NCAA championships in 2014 and 2015.

The *Los Lobos de Loyola* sculpture, designed by Mexican artist Pancho Cardenas, was unveiled on Wolf and Kettle Day 2012, a day celebrating the generosity of the Loyola community. Legend has it that the Loyola family was so successful that after feeding their family and soldiers, they had enough food to feed the animals. This act of giving is represented by the two wolves and kettle depicted on Loyola's shield.

The Alfie Norville Practice Facility, named in honor of trustee and alum Allan Norville's late wife, Alfena, opened in 2018 and provides much-needed practice space for the men's and women's basketball and volleyball teams. Built to Silver-LEED standards, the building features a green roof, permeable paving landscaping, and energy-efficient heating and cooling. A skywalk connects the Alfie to the Norville Center.

Baumhart Hall, a new 25-story residence hall on Loyola's Water Tower Campus, opened to students in 2006. Named for Loyola's longest-serving president, Raymond C. Baumhart, SJ, it features 168 apartments, a food court, a university chapel, 24-hour security, and close proximity to Loyola's School of Law, the Quinlan School of Business, and the School of Communication.

In 2009, the 16-story building known as 25 East Pearson at the Water Tower Campus, which is now the home of the School of Law, was renamed the Philip H. Corboy Law Center after alumnus Philip H. Corboy (School of Law, class of 1949). Corboy's generous gifts provided for student scholarships and major renovations, including a new mock courtroom named for Philip Corboy's father, Robert J. Corboy.

In 2015, a new home for Loyola's Quinlan School of Business opened at 16 East Pearson Street, the John and Kathy Schreiber Center. Named for alumnus John Schreiber (class of 1970) and his wife, Kathy, this 10-story Gold-LEED building features the Gorman Family Great Stairs on the first floor, modeled after the Spanish Steps in Rome.

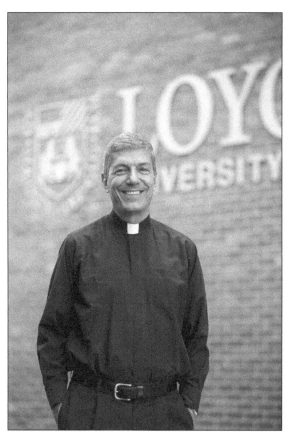

Recognizing a need to provide equitable education, Loyola president Michael J. Garanzini, SJ, decided to open a two-year college at Loyola to provide associate degree programs for students with limited financial resources but with an interest in attending a four-year university following graduation. Arrupe College, named for Pedro Arrupe, SJ, the former father general of the Society of Jesus, opened on the Water Tower Campus in 2015. Founding dean and executive director Fr. Steve Kastsouros, SJ, created an environment where students received intensive one-on-one contact with faculty and holistic support while earning associate degrees that can easily transfer to state and private universities. Arrupe College offers associate degrees in art and humanities, business, and social and behavioral sciences with a strategy to allow low-income students to fully fund instruction with financial aid and accumulation of little to no debt.

The first Arrupe College class graduated in 2017, holding its commencement ceremony in Mundelein Auditorium on the Lake Shore Campus. The event marked a milestone for the college and its 82 graduates. Cook County board president Toni Preckwinkle gave the inaugural commencement address. Seventy-three of the graduates reported they would be pursuing further education to earn bachelor's degrees at colleges and universities around the country.

The School of Communication, established in 2009, moved into the new building at 51 East Pearson Street on the Water Tower Campus in December 2009. The school offers state-of-the-art, on-site production facilities, labs, and equipment and is home to Loyola's WLUW, a 24-hour FM radio station, and the *Phoenix*, the award-winning student newspaper. Adjacent to the School of Communication is the Clare, a high-rise senior independent living community.

In 1997, the Stritch School of Medicine moved into a new medical education building on the Maywood campus. The facility provides infrastructure for many curricular innovations, such as a three-year patient-centered medicine curriculum and an online educational bioethics program through the Neiswanger Institute for Bioethics & Health Policy. In 2001, the building was renamed the John and Herta Cuneo Center, in recognition of their generous support of medical education.

On September 6, 2017, Loyola medical students protested the repeal of the DACA program at the Stritch School of Medicine. The school was and is an active supporter of the DREAM Act, which allowed students to enroll in education programs regardless of their immigration status. (Photograph courtesy of Mark G. Kuczweksi, PhD, HEC-C, director, Neiswanger Institute for Bioethics & Health Policy, Loyola University Chicago.)

In July 2017, the DREAM Act legislation was introduced in the US Senate. During October 2017, a total of 2,454 members of Loyola's community sent 7,362 letters to 84 senators and 297 US representatives in support of the act. As a Jesuit institution, Loyola University Chicago firmly believes in the dignity of each person and in the promotion of social justice.

The new Marcella Niehoff School of Nursing building opened on the Maywood campus in late 2012. The new building houses the Walgreen Family Virtual Hospital, with six clinical simulation labs that allow students to practice collaborative care of adult, pediatric, obstetric, and geriatric patients and the Galante Information Commons, an electronic health sciences library for all faculty and students.

Loyola's Center for Translational Research and Education opened on the Maywood campus in April 2016. The 225,000-square-foot building is the largest and most complex building in university history and serves the Stritch School of Medicine, the Graduate School, Marcella Niehoff School of Nursing, and Loyola University Health Systems. The center features a bridge connecting the Cardinal Bernardin Cancer Center and state-of-the-art wet and dry research laboratories.

Loyola welcomed its inaugural class in the Parkinson School of Health Sciences and Public Health at its Lake Shore and Maywood Campuses in 2019. Beginning with six programs from the Niehoff School of Nursing and the Stritch School of Medicine, founding dean Dr. Elaine Morrato plans eventual expansion to 16 programs. Alumni Robert L. and Elizabeth M. Parkinson gave the lead gift for the establishment of the school.

In 2009, Loyola purchased the Monte Mario property for the John Felice Rome Center campus, a five-acre property on a hill northwest of Vatican City and the center of Rome. In December 2004, Michael J. Garanzini, SJ, Loyola president, dedicated the center to its founder, John Felice. The John Felice Rome Center offers a variety of courses for students, including classical civilization, fine arts, film, music, fashion, architecture, sculpture, communication, political science, history, literature, philosophy, and business, as well as opportunities for internships and service-learning. Students have the option to study for a full academic year or just the summer session.

The John Felice Rome Center (JFRC) encourages students to look beyond the Rome campus while studying abroad. Students have an opportunity to take excursion trips to Greece, Poland, the western Balkans, and other locations in Europe. Loyola has added another option for studying abroad by becoming the first American university to have a study abroad program in Vietnam. Located in Ho Chi Minh City, the Vietnam Center offers two academic specializations, Environmental Challenges Facing our World: Vietnam and the Environment and Global Business and Entrepreneurship in Southeast Asia. Internships and service-learning placements are available at the Vietnam Center, as at the JFRC. Loyola encourages students to take advantage of these study abroad programs to foster an appreciation of global diversity and expand their worldviews.

In 2009, the Cuneo Foundation, the family foundation of John and Herta Cuneo, gave the Cuneo mansion and gardens to Loyola. Located in Vernon Hills, the mansion was completed in 1916 as the home of Samuel Insull. In 1937, John Cuneo Sr. bought the mansion for his wife and two children. Today, it offers a space for events and courses from Loyola's continuing education program.

In 2010, Loyola purchased the 98-acre Resurrection Retreat Center in Woodstock from the Congregation of the Resurrection and renamed it the Loyola University Retreat and Ecology Campus. It offers a unique setting for conferences, retreats, workshops, classes, and special events. The mission of the campus is to be a place for spiritual and intellectual growth through retreats and for study and research of the environment and ecological sustainability.

BIBLIOGRAPHY

Felice, John P. and Mary K. Felice. *The Rome Center, 1962–1976*. Unpublished manuscript, 1976.

Loyola University Alumni Directory, 1919.

Loyola University Chicago Archives & Special Collections.
    Thomas J. Bryant, SJ, Photograph Collection, 1958–1979.
    Thomas J. Dyba Photograph Collection, 1950–1963.
    Stanley Fahlstrom, MD, Papers, 1942–1947.
    William T. Kane, SJ, Collection, 1829–1945.
    Office of the President Records, 1858–1980.
    Reference File Collection.
    St. Bernard's School of Nursing Fonds, 1906–1975.
    Joe Smajo Photograph Collection, 1950–1958.
    University Photograph Collection.
    University Portrait Collection.

Roubik, Joseph. *Loyola University at Seventy*. Unpublished manuscript, 1943.

INDEX

Business, School of, 68, 116, 117

Commerce, College of, 47, 53, 55, 57, 58

Dental Department, 81, 82

Dentistry, School of, 7, 8, 69, 79–88

Downtown College, 53–55, 57–59

John Felice Rome Center, 8, 97, 98, 108, 109, 123, 124, 126

Lake Shore Campus, 7, 8, 17–52, 60, 61, 93, 96, 109–116, 122

Law, School of, 7, 8, 18, 35, 45, 53–58, 66–68, 116, 117

Medical Campus, 7, 8, 69–96, 109, 120–122

Medicine, School of, 7, 8, 58, 69–79, 91, 109, 120–122

Nursing, School of, 7, 8, 39, 69, 79, 89–96, 121, 122, 126

Niehoff School of Nursing, 7, 8, 39, 69, 95, 96, 121, 122

Rome Center, 7, 8, 97–109, 123, 124, 126

Social Work, School of, 7, 8, 35, 53, 56, 66

St. Ignatius College, 7–18, 23, 25, 27, 36, 54, 69

Stritch School of Medicine, 7, 8, 69, 76, 79, 80, 88, 109, 120–122

Water Tower Campus, 8, 48, 53–68, 109, 116–119

Visit us at
arcadiapublishing.com

Lightning Source UK Ltd.
Milton Keynes UK
UKHW050335020323
417864UK00004B/138